Calamity's Quilt

Calamity's Quilt

Janet I. Buck

With an introduction by
Thomas Fortenberry

Newton's Baby
Scottdale, Georgia

Printed in Canada

Published in the United States of America by

Newton's Baby
788 Murphey Street
Scottdale, GA 30079

First Edition, December 1999

The Newton's Baby Contemporary Poetry Series, Volume 2

Library of Congress Card Number: 99-067975

ISBN 0-9667228-4-1

Cover art and design by Cheryl Hight Carle

Some poems in this collection were first published in the following journals: Gravity, The Melic Review, Mind Fire, Athens City Times, Indie Journal, Kimera, The Oracular Tree, ApparentDepth, A Room without Walls, Maelstrom, Poetry Heaven, Serpentine, New Thought Journal, Poetic Peaches & Dreams, Sapphire Magazine, The Poetry Kit, Thought Cafe, A Writer's Choice, Pogonip, Locust Magazine, Thunder Sandwich, Poetik License, Poet's Cut, San Francisco Salvo, Ygdrasil, Perceptions, Lynx: Poetry from Bath, Pigs 'n Poets, the storyteller, INKBLOTS Magazine, Miserere, Burn Online, PoetryRepairShop, The Green Tricycle, BeeHive, silentium amoris, Beaded Strand, The Part-time Postmodernist, Niederngasse, The Horsethief's Journal, Carved in Sand, Poetry Super Highway and The Rose & Thorn.

In Dedication to Mark—

who taught me how sad
the sin of silence is

Table of Contents

Introduction

I was very pleased when I first saw the title chosen for Janet Buck's debut book. Nothing could be more apt. My late grandmother, Syble, created quilts all her life. I still have several she made for me. They are patchworks of memory. Quilts are special things, irreplaceable works made by hand and stitched with love and caring attention to detail. Each quilt is very unique and tells a different story. That Janet's quilt is a quilt of calamity is fitting. Calamities, whether large or small, whether natural or man-made, are what shape our lives. Storms and divorces destroy homes; diseases and jealousy destroy lives. We all experience calamities to one degree or another. But I do not fear calamities. Calamities are good things, for they weather and texture our souls, build our character, and shape our destinies. Our lives are thus proverbial quilts sewn with the patches of survival torn from our various calamities. This book is a testament of calamity, a Dante-esque journey down and back again (in her words "scratching suffer's fingernails / against the promise of light"), and the unbelievable power of Janet's victory in life.

Janet Buck writes from life, from reality. Her writing is not cutesy workshop exercises or flowery language for the sake of rhymes and romantic looks, but just the opposite. This is unflinching experience. It is raw emotion poured forth, calmly recollected just enough that Wordsworth would have been proud, but still so edgy it is unsettling. It is written with a strength and validity that is not learned and only comes from the debt of living fully. Every syllable of this text is earned.

The best part of reading Buck is that her writing is honest. It is the real deal. You will find an infinity of moments captured here. This cannot be faked. Thus, not only is she is a writer's writer, but she is required reading for the living. Janet Buck is a writer to respect.

It was an honor to be asked to write this foreword for a number of reasons. One, she is someone I deeply respect. Not simply because she is a fabulous poet, but moreover because of her character. She is simply amazing. Janet is as trustworthy and true a friend as can be found. She is what people call a good person. That is a rarity these days— a precious gem. Secondly, we have a little history together. I discovered her as both a reader and an editor, that is from the sides of pleasure and work at the same time. I was doubly satisfied. I have watched her develop online, a new voice in a new medium. She has grown up with the World Wide Web, so to speak. In fact, she has become so successful at it, that now she is a pillar of the online literary community. This moment is a joy for me. It is both a favorite poet's coming of age and the recognition of a dear friend's great ability.

Now, a word for her. Janet, you remind us not to take life for granted. You remind us to enjoy every breathtaking second of it and live each moment to the fullest. In this way you are a natural teacher. You teach us the painful conquest of each step, the bitter joy of every breath, the precious gift of every word. Thank you for the lessons, my friend.

Thomas Fortenberry
August 15, 1999
Charlotte, NC

Thomas Fortenberry is an editor and writer of nonfiction, fiction, poetry, comic books, plays, teleplays, and screenplays. He edits the literary magazines Mind Fire, Phic-shun, Maelstrom, Soul Unmade, Morphiseum, and The Southerner. He has a degree in history and currently resides in Charlotte, NC, with his family.

Calamity's Quilt

I Spell-check Will

Color me not with your eyes for
poison pancreatic tears haunt gray sky
as ribbons of a Nazi flag.
You call the Red Sea of my bed
a smooth and scarlet holocaust.
My day is an ordinary
clothesline of challenges:
I splatter coffee on the rug,
shake it off as hunting dogs;
lips, hips, crutches I despise,
with a fever known only to death;
I spell-check will, hop awkward
toward a swimming pool.
Chlorine is trapped in my hair
like bubble gum, but I love its scent,
for it tells me that I have moved
like a chessboard bishop
over pawns of strife.

A refugee of writing's camp.
Cactus concentration mourns
the plastic dolls of easy street.
Underground beneath my flesh—
keyboard fingers growing wet
like soggy crackers dipped in soup.
It's liver soap that cleanses pain,
rappelling cliffs of just one shoe.
I ride the camel sitting up,
traversing Himalayan scars.
You read their crusts, feel their breeze,
a soundtrack for a courage horn.
This pilgrimage, a pyramid.
My bricks just grateful rocks in wells.
Minor issues: scorpions.
Little things: tarantulas.
Stanzas born of tended stings.
My life a pregnant oyster shell.

Frowning Clowns

My legs, a pair of frowning clowns
with noses long as Cyrano's.
Scuba gear of poetry:
rubber condoms, measured, sold
in footprints of a rolling chair.
Slow saxophones with drying reeds.
Kissing concrete more than not.
I wanted knees of napkin rings—
linen sexy pressed in place.
Not rhapsodies of blue despair
or tubas chasing agony.

Move is juicy nectarines.
Flesh, one wide and borrowed bruise.
My headsets are your fairy tales,
floor shows minus ticket stubs.
They plug themselves in
sockets of my guarded eyes.
Standing after surgery,
an anthem brought to roiling boils.
The hamstring of an absent limb
is not a braided courage myth,
but knitting needles sliding fast—
wooden spoons in burning skillets—
caught in crusted laps of ill.

Motion drops another stitch.
My stump, a pornographic bomb
announcing life is never fair.
Your medicine just chases pins—
puts them back at panic time.
Before the mine of mimic blows—
becomes the only shining light.
Born of one long strand mistake
and artificial bobby pins,
I poke mad holes in pantyhose.
The baby's breath of hope attached,
a garland taped to thinning hair.

Well-intended Trinities

Ice on lips of slick cement:
an equal sign for closing doom.
I walked corpse-stiff against the wall
as if a cliff were on my tail.
Swimming stood for paradise
and paradox of motion's threat.
Muscles cleaved by hammer knives
could not survive another fall.
A well-intended trinity appeared
and spread help's tablecloth—
its lily bloomed the very second
crutch tips crippled hit the room.

They brought three chairs (all at once).
The burst of pity's synergy.
I shrunk from aid like woolen socks
in water boiled by crossbone fires.
Their kindness should have read caress,
but sandpaper flaws were in my face.
Attentiveness was stocking caps
on burglars pinned by pistols drawn.
The accidental favor launched:
a trespass to my eyes alone.
Riven limbs are private stashes,
open gashes, secret ashes
stacked and sorted in the dark.
Platitudes came popping out
from ice-trays of such willing hearts;
the part they didn't realize
was how the freeze had stuck to tongues
and ways a Venus sculpture moves
to dodge tarantulas of eyes
in hot tubs full of scorpions.

Phyllo Flesh

Let's come clean.
I hate my legs.
Right: reduced to almost nothing.
Left: a frozen carrot,
whittled by scathing eyes
'til its surface ice
turns to sand I can sweep.
There is no one to blame.
Just fate
waxing floors.
Luck slipped.
Just fate
pouring rocks in the soap.
When I wash the flesh
of honest worms,
they tear like sheets of phyllo
on the nut-*sweet*-meat of art.

It's really *sweat*, but I shall
not argue the point,
because I must write.
Fight my way upstream toward pride.
This is, yup, the hardest poem
I've ever done.
Feeding blood to the leeches
on the spit-shined shore
of an ivory page.
Proofing is impossible so typos stay—
poured fast in concrete seas.
"I hate my legs. I like my words."
"I hate my legs. I like my words."
Coyotes on a rage with owls.
Bat wings echo in a cave.
I fill the cups of shadows
with dark, dark darts.
Right! Left! Write!
So, this is how a poet howls.

Depressing Wheels

Limping right behind the pain
of wearing thin mobility.
I watch you move like beavers
calling stones to them for
building dams, enduring days.
One arm on the grocery cart.
The other on depressing wheels.
Back and forth maneuvering.
It is the dance of fate askew.

Tires more like rubber bands.
Stretch too far. Your health will snap.
Granted toes belong to others
sunning on the come and stay
of bones that do what they are told
and follow wishes of the mind.
In the chair was "in my face."
A cobra in the jungle fever
sweating, very sweating truth.
Sunk so low. Distilling eyes.
Change the focus with a smile.
Move your stares to other skies.
Drink the fire of gratitude
and leave my aching soul alone.

You thought my eyes belonged
with theirs, but nothing's further
from the truth. I know the
clench of agony and legs
like soggy carrot sticks.
The rusted valves of irony.
Those who see the lace of life
are rocking on its brittle edge.

Mincemeat Bones

Dishpan hands of moving quills
that wipe the counter clean of shame.
Hamburger Hill without the guns.
Will sticks out its iron tongue;
soap gets in the eyes of try.
The fox-trot of a fake leg
is not a Steinway,
nor a Schubert waltz.
If it were, it isn't tuned.
The midget of faith
and mincemeat bones
have no sugar in their crusts.

Sitting soggy down to write,
I always fear the civilized
will call the setting pity's clouds
or carousels of weak retorts
that slow like aging music boxes
wound and sighing with their greed.
The girth and girdle of the pain
that leaves a bedsore on my hands.
I sharpen scissors of a poem
and live embodied in the curse.
Know circus tents of cardboard skirts
will never change the climate's mud.
Their stakes will slip
on slick-tongued floors—
you'll touch bad luck like patches
of clover in summertime grass;
in the end, my wax will melt;
cotton balls of whiter lives
will wear thick clots of bitter blood.

In Search of Grace

The movie* played liked battered tapes;
I was filling in its wings.
Starring rugged Robert Redford,
pieces of a little girl.
Her name was "Grace" (ironically)
in search of all her grace removed.
The horse (called Pilgrim)
once a stallion fixed for hope.
Camera jolts from hooves to feet—
the nervous twitch of realize
cutting through a Hallmark card.

Post-accident in waiting rooms:
emotion, stretching trampolines
on bongo drums without a score.
Post-amputation's horror flick
in solipsistic monologues.
I saw my own life screaming there:
wondered how my parents coped
with walls like wax on balance beams.
I watched her touch her brace with eyes—
practice climbing normal stairs.
Lament epiphanies of shame
that halter motion's syllables.

Panting breaths of confidence
work their way through
softened scars, but never
do explain their points—
arrows on a weather vane
with targets of imbedded skies.
Ipso facto accident that almost
put a horse to sleep.
Together in a stinking stable
scratching suffer's fingernails
against the promise of the light.

****The Horse Whisperer***, starring Robert Redford and Kristin Scott Thomas, 1998.

Acrylic Thighs

A long, lewd list of serpents perched
on bitter curves of screaming walls—
finches on a wire charged
with fate's intrinsic accident.
Take your pick off morbid's menu.
Tongues in quicksand of their coils.
Every year I taste yet more.
In terms of knives.
Of geographic carpet lice.
Split infinitives of grief
cling like leeches to my skin.
Medicine records the rape
but doesn't change its chemistry.

I meet the ground with sloppy fear
like cold potatoes dumped on tile.
Will's tight kleptomaniac that
eats through plates of Styrofoam.
I seem to miss move's dinner bell.
Spell out wind chimes of the Fall.
Suffer's time on Satan's lap.
The gap between our earthly folds:
me, myself, acrylic thighs
with metal pipes—
relentless and unmovable
as cacti on a desert's floor.

The Tapeworm

I trespass into trouble zones.
Forks I've used have two
bent prongs: liquor's lightbulb
was the first; the second
was a crossing guard of poetry—
a riverbed of clever owls
that howl in a forest blessed.
Sometimes playing satin pillows;
sometimes hot electric chairs.
Book reports of battle grounds—
harpoons stabbing squirming sharks.
You're wondering about that worm.
A silent crematorium that
takes command of what it sees.
Always in the pinching mode
like toothpicks in a voodoo doll.

Armor of esprit de corps
will always rattle with the night.
The essence of aesthetics honest
grinding chills of history.
I laminate a scorching sun—
reminders and remainders call.
Feel my way like orange peels
that float Venetian tidal pools.
Passing neat unlettered whim—
kidney stones that search for sand
around a birth I thought I knew
but never really truly met.
Listen for the hollow suction
gripping every human heart.
Sparklers of a syllable
I launch and trace remote control.
Moons drop light like boxers shorts
around a messy alphabet.

Garbage Ties Around Long Reefs

My body's doom: hauling
six-packs up steep hills—
storms from sick's Mt. Everest.
Guffawing winds. Goliath will.
Hoping that their holes won't spread,
I wrap up limbs for garbage bags—
assure myself I want that climb
like rainbows over prison camps.
The pedal, to you, is one of two
with cutesy rhymes in puzzled place.
Predictable as grainy salt
that takes its stand in passing waves.

To me, it's tapping blind white canes.
Feeling earth through glassy loss.
Each step I spend is freedom shared
with poverty: a bubble bath of $10 bills.
I put my pain pills in the drawer—
spasm as I mount our bike.
It's always an unmetered ride
in pastures of perhapsing falls.
Sitting idle's trading
places with condemned.
Motion's sights in pirate shock,
I know how big that ocean is.

The Ivory Cane

Packing up the winter rage
and laying out my summer clothes.
This would be the very last
of chewing wicks in broken candles
rolling in the bottom of drawer
of hopping to identity.
I would write of romping puppies.
Button-noses. Marigolds.
The perma-press of mere accepting.
Stanzas steaming wrinkled shirts.

Strains of pains that hammer
stammer even when I punish them
and tell them to behave themselves.
The blasts of plaster body casts
that crackled as I touched their creases.
Canasta clapping slapping,
tapping, strapping, napping
wet amalgams of this analyzing.
Skipping like a broken record
over scratches in my mind.

I would buy a pair of jeans.
Wear them 'til the fit was final
on these dregs of driftwood bones.
Letting go was, well, removing
hooks from all the squirming poles
and fishing for the pearl buttons
caught between the couch's cushions.
Time to tummy-tuck the missing.
Trade these olive pits for sane.
Coming home to art was hard.
Combing crowded parking lots
and hunting for the perfect slot.
A victim of internal shadows
walking with an ivory cane.

Sardine Slippers

In the orchestra pit
of acceptable dreams,
crippled flesh is dirty snow.
Its stench is unforgettable—
like grass clippings
stashed in a closed garage
or peat moss on carpets
of a brand new truck.
We hang storms
as thick as bedroom drapes.
Difference dandruff is rebuffed,
as if its arsenic capabilities
are a contact sport and
the game is coming to a close.

Slugs and snails of falling tears
are fingerprints on coffee mugs.
Flyers of mortality's presence
stuck uninvited under wiper blades.
Emotion's pollen (of course)
requires a tuba to clear
its passageways
and limping parades
are hard to watch
since whacked off legs
don't grow back and
courage stripes seldom see
the war dissolve.
So we all waltz avoiding—
pretending we don't.
Sardine slippers of perhaps
I'm next, well, determine
the direction of Gestapo eyes.

The Bathroom Scale

For years, your eyes have been
my bathroom scale—
I weigh too much. We both know that.
Afraid that I'll bring
the world down a step,
rather than take it up
a fraction of an inch,
I have not told you the truth
or shared my ghosts.
My stump is a clenched fist
with the wiggle of worms.
Clover's poise is beards shaved
that do not grow back
when I stumble and fall.
My gait is a prick in velvet flesh.
I speak too loud. I sober trite.

Crutches, chairs, and metal parts
are trappings of my destiny,
moved around with care and dread.
To you, they're logs that scratch white paint.
To me, just pretzels rolled in salt
in a brown-bag lunch I didn't choose.
In me, you see the zap of limits
like a lobster plunged in a boiling pot.
My body parts are cracked crab backs—
wash down shores and leave distress.
Stitches and scars are giant weeds,
cattails stranded in a ditch.
I reach for wreaths of motion's gift
despite the tics of thorns on blessed.

Bankrupt Bones

Bankrupt bones push silently
so losing health is a slow
but very real rape.
Stolen purse Unfortunatus
screams its issues constantly.
The czar and king of courage scratch—
pit bulls warming up their teeth.
Effort's abbot is a robot
taking charge of grocery aisles.
Every foot I think of planting
takes expensive conference calls.
Calibrated urgency whistles
motion's crucial moon.

Your fiery tongue of curious
lights on leg-less like a leech—
stays as lice when I collapse.
I dread disaster à la mode,
but wear it as a wedding gown.
Epidemic set apart—
anemic draining confidence.
You didn't need to set me straight.
From summer gardens of your eyes
and fences up around your lies,
I know I match a broken chair.
I know that I was born a weed.

Trading Places

Pre-Op stretching.
Tapes rewinding.
Cedar strength uprooted.
Slaughtered hoofs of recall
padding into nauseating caves
and swollen heels stuck
on stepping stones of rage.
Strangers wishing well
with potted plants
and greeting cards
of euphemism plastered over
frozen reservoirs of dread.

Rolling gurneys.
Sterile air.
Suspended moment.

Post-Op pounding.
Ethered lungs and tethered hands
that know too well
the gaping gown of naked fear
and clotted streams of will.
Lips of envelopes
that fail to seal
despite the wetted tongue
of stoic prattle.

Breathing tied to belts of pain
and threaded through the loops
of every passing moment.
Bones and muscles of betrayal
wanting scripts rewritten.

Those who flip you adages
like "Well, the worst is over now"
never had to climb the stairs
or feel the thirst for guarantees
of touching toes
and walking pastures of perspective.

For Jeannette

Harm's Way

In short Haikus, my whittled limbs
will teach you things
with apoplectic certainty.
Their crawlspace is so limited,
they trim the fat off easy meat.
Rattled brainwaves of a tear;
tumble at the slightest trauma
breaking concentration's tail.

I've earned a right to moodiness,
but hate that state of mind
so much, I'd rather live
in busy fits of fast denial
than wear solicitude of weak.
Sumptuary laws of pride
determine effort's solemn shape.
Struggle is one floating plight
infecting every way I turn—
but I would kiss it
French-tongue style
in lieu of losing art of motion
even in its limping curse.

Harm's way fashions repertoires
of ugly shame, but also stacks
thick courage bricks.
I study hard discomfort
of the universe;
scratch firm trouble in my shorts.
The sex of one successful step
behind the rocks of ones collapsed.
Try's mortar is a muted
shade but never moot.
Its firm erection rules the earth.

Pajama Feet

The litany and liturgy of
cotton flannel luxuries
would always be a demon here.
A slap upside my fated cheeks.
Rubbing acetone on *Q-tips*.
Slipping them in open wounds.
Crutches were a crappie easel
turning out a huge mistake.
Pajamas in a Christmas box
were tubas chasing agony.

They told me what I did not own.
Underlined with felt-tip pens
the ways of graceful bouncing checks.
Feet they wore were made of art:
a child's Michelangelo.
Stained-glass lucky on the ceiling.
Dropping what was clearly missing
at my foot that should have been
at least a plural entity.
Flat balloons of trouser legs
wore penis envy of a sort.
Flour sacks of empty caverns
begging for a place to hide.
Dante's dolls with china faces
sitting on a screaming wall.

Advising Rats

Asphyxiated by the night of
living in a wheelchair.
The evidence coincidence.
You are there by force of fate.
I am on the edge of mobile.
Hanging on like slaughtered birds
to wires of experience
I know have crossed in skeletons
and skulls apparent under
mounds of doctor bills.

You are homeless. I am not.
Desperation comes in flavors
all mixed up in anger's soup.
The sign your other half has posted:
"Will Will Will
Will Work for Food."
You chat like hens in busy yards,
just watching traffic pass you by.
I am driving Easy Street
and want to stop, but God
it's hard to tell if I would simply
make the evening's cloud of pity
turn a very hated shade of black.

I think I'd be an imposition.
Mats unwelcome. Very envied.
Advising rats are dimes in dozens.
Every window rolling up like
drawing bridges to a castle
in advance of treasures lost.
I have been to lucky wells
of money falling from the stars.
Inheriting a stubborn streak
but also ways to help me walk.

We will always know too well
the rows of eyes asphyxiating
every muscle trying like
the devil's angel oxymoron
flying through an empty sky.
A rainbow will erase our lives
and we will go down under
battles others never have to see.

The chalk on boards of
tragic lives is dust to some.
For many it is merely mold.
I use you like an empty page
retaining where I might have gone.
Why is justice fast asleep?
I almost vomit gratitude.
See my feeble bones as blessings,
almost Band-Aids of the dawn.

The Surgery

Coming to in hours split
like fences with their nails raw.
The clots of blood they left behind.
Jelly no one wanted
on their nervous hands.
Skin like toast they turned
to hide the crusts of pain.
The sighs in curtains of their eyes
that read: "The slug of death
was here and left a trail
in tire tracks upon her naked flesh."

Coming to and crawling out.
Arms in ditches by the rails.
The shots she welcomed like the rain that
follows deserts baking in the scorching sun.
Her brothers brought a case of beer.
Played with buttons on their shirts.
Hawaiian prints like traitors to the dark
they tried to ride and surf beyond.

Stale sheets, the wedding trains
that eager feet were stepping on.
Rapunzel in a tower made of bars
with sewer pipes and razor blades.
Her honey tresses clipped like grass.
Soaking wet with shaking off
the places she had been.
Like cats that children corner
in the night and try to dress.
The scratch is one that didn't fade.

The Spiral Staircase

I climb you stairs for no other reason
than concrete knowledge
that I cannot stand to fail.
Three avenues beseech my bones:
the stairs, the elevator cage,
and the immiscible chair.
I've stripped the latter's paint
even though I have not worn its presence,
as mud slides toward immobile go.
With swollen will and heaving lungs,
disapproval's beriberi scorching
the drapes of my limping ways
in a war known only to those
who have parted with legs.

A kamikaze pilot in a diving plane
that draws his strength from panic winds,
the mission of "try" is all I know.
Spiral stares, the other kind,
ones I turn my back to face,
are Texas twisters to my mind.
So let's pretend, for a sliver of time,
that I shall roll the egg of suffer
from the countertop and catch it smartly
in advance of the crash.

Indubitably, this wet denial is turpentine
that etherizes accidental falls.
My bones, like splattered pigeons' wings,
lie in seas of toppled stones—
sugar on a spoon
I must lick before it dries.
Determination's shiny Packard
on the showroom floor
of a swimming pool,
I work this anger out and float.

Whale Bones

Crutches seem like scrimshaw art.
All this talk of loving self—
bookends sliding down a shelf.
A busy beach with running feet
is reading *Playgirl* on the john.
My awkward feels like
taking hammers to a screw.
Talk of taping wedding days
would turn my difference inside out—
lines around a body bag
without a proper burial.

Looking straight at bathroom mirrors—
quite the disappointing fax.
To have my limp on video,
a violation of the dawn
with copper shadows of the ways
my shape will never measure up.
Martial artless of a fall
where confidence goes quickly bald—
wings collapse before they fly.
Effort's oatmeal dries so thick—
that tape would turn to sticks of gum.
All those sexy fairy tales
seem so crazy out of place
like bridal gowns with tennis shoes
or serving eggnog in July.

Coming To

In agony.
With arms like daffodils in June
that hadn't seen a drop of rain.
Legs like flour sacks
they heaved and tossed upon the bed.
Corners of the sterile sheets.
Papercuts that slice the night
and drench it with the blood of tears.

"Cheer Up! My God!
You might have Died!"
Missing what it was to hear
the rooster of the empty space
and all the things they might have said
that pounded in her ears.

Pitchforks of the hollow eyes
she buried with a smile.
Seas of masks above her head.
Pillows fluffed on pity's couch
they fingered time and time again.
Like rosaries without a plan
to carry off the pain.

Rolling in like limousines
with squeaking brakes
that didn't think before they spoke.
The times she wanted nothing
but her father's arms
to pack the days like broken plates
and haul them to the dump.

The Botticelli Bottlebrush

There are secrets of the universe to be learned from people who have nothing. I've lived with them and it's dirty and smelly, but very ***rich****.*
--Mitch Longley

Age five. Long face.
Its leather almost husks of corn.
She sat on floors I'd memorized.
I wanted so to shorten them.
Looking up at rows of legs
from margins of a missing one.
Aware health's fortune is a myth
where wise is just fermented pain.
Her plastic leg in seams of shame—
I knew them better than my skin.
A lobster trapped in tanks of eyes
shelling time and growing up
in very unexpected ways.

Socratic oaths of oafish steps that
buy their way up flights of stairs.
Languid sense in cotton balls
beneath bright lies she'd learn to use—
paper tape on bandages—
sirens on an ambulance
ward off demons hauling grief.
I wanted to share cool hiccups
of forests I'd learned to part.
Separate like whites and darks
with licenses of feeble words.
Its pillow was a rusted tractor
bringing in a stack of hay.
To tell her—bones of *Brillo Pads*
could not escape a grimy sink.

There are no clouds of cashmere tears,
but candor's whisk works better
than denial's sweep with eyelash
brooms that blink at dust and miss
thick waves of scenery.

Tapioca trouble time that grew
dessert from feeble rice.
A Botticelli bottlebrush
that finds a way to carve its shape
in seaweed threads of absent art.

Dante's Dolls

Your bones have Gershwin elegance.
Mine are twigs and broken toothpicks.
Spots in Dante's doll collection
running on adrenaline.
My flesh in scars and often scraps,
crimps in pie crust cast aside.
Still they do coyote howls
in circles of a courage moon.

As you run free,
you watch me limp.
The tremor of imbalance loud
as Parkinson in nursing homes.
My angel wings are heroes crushed
like flaming butts of old cigars.
The scent of leather in my hair
does not emerge from horsy rides,
but belts and screws and super-glue
on feisty joints that think
somehow the sun will shine.

Bars on windows of my soul
are only spread by poetry.
If you glared at me in naked truth
at Christmas parties
dancing awkward from the booze,
I'd show you tickets of dismissal.
Hide in wreaths of cosmic smiles.
There are borders to this honesty.
Deserts I'll not let you cross.
Agony's a publication;
still lifes of a cloistered war.

The Eye Patch

Blinders on a rocking horse,
the page does what it wills
with what I've lost.
Misfit marches trapped in gauze.
The Barbie leg they pin to me—
grabs at grace and finds a ditch
for bowls of morning cereal.

In "Screw You" mode,
we ride a tandem mountain bike.
I pedal its rose without my limb.
Tongues hang out like puppies
panting thirstily.
Cross between pain's blood and bliss.
Thighs confusing homonyms.

Reflectors on a cycle's wheels,
I bring your mortal base to halts.
Rolling thrones of wheelchairs
would drop my heart in toilet bowls.
What a mammoth aching shame.
To never hop the length of dreams.

I click through climbs like lousy gears.
If you watch my face—
ignore my legs—you'll see
how wind combs matted hair.
How Moses drew his tapping cane,
marveled at the size of earth
when spirit scaled some mountain top.

Pity's Prozac

The subject was the wheelchair.
Here we sat so far apart.
Head to comprehending head.
Missing toe to missing toe.
The cavity beneath the sky was
one that's hit a pocket wind.
I felt like *Jell-O* bouncing fast
in bellies of a crashing plane.

The stewardess was fate, of course.
And we were drinking pity's wind.
You were fifty.
I was sixteen guns of fire.
Saluting what it was to dream and
sail beyond like clipper ships
with destinations of a smile.
You were young enough, I thought,
to drink the foam of tragedy
and live to spit it out again.
Fifty isn't over just
because you have a missing limb.

Somehow I was jasmine tea
that offered very sweet replies
of reciprocity in faith.
I showed you mine and walked
the halls like elephants in circus tents
that lead the show without a choice.
I think it's best explained with this:
I was horny for a life. And you,
my friend, could feel the pulse
like undertows beneath the waves
of something called an inner-voice.

An Argument Ad Hominem

Poverty was a doll collection
we passed in a Porsche.
A bicycle race with a roaring train—
its victories beyond contend.
A roll of film in bottom drawers.
Developing was buried here
and suffer tried to bring it out.
Polluted spirits have a smell;
noses aren't the temples
or the churches they once were.

A man fell from the back
of a pick-up truck like a
cardboard box that blows
away from lack of weight.
His bonsai chest had blackened moss.
Blood ran thick as dripping wax.
Bamboo shoots of arms seemed lost.
His beard and lashes rolled in grease
of bars of soap so out of reach.
We all passed by this homeless,
curdled hopelessness
(locked our automatic doors)
as quickly, as deftly, as sadly
as a shutter's predictable click.
A *Robin Hood* perhaps.
But poorer than the movie kind.
A statistical Christ that
had no slot in tax returns.
Despite the fact his body
was an argument *ad hominem*
for saving flesh of someone's son.

City Snow

A warm June day and still it snowed.
Ice-cubes were the people kind.
Sad and laugh-less in the city's colon.
Skies that somehow scraped themselves
like razors rusted by the humid.
Bumper anxious seemed to spread.
We came to play in party bunkers.
Didn't know there would be war.
Traffic was a backed-up toilet.
Clouds of smoke in bitter puffs.
A car just, wham, exploded
merely feet away from us.
Fire hoses stretched the streets
like arms and legs of rattlesnakes.
The body empty. Black and gray
as old briquettes that begged
forgetting flames to burn.
Sunday morning news on pasted screens
in lobbies full of busy ants
without a hill or destination.

Melon skins of people sandwiched.
City indigestion twisting: "A man was
murdered yesterday...beaten, tied, and dragged
by ropes to rolling wheels on gravel roads.
Wonder who we should have blamed..."
No one in the lobby moved.
The justice eyebrow to be plucked.
Ingrown hairs of such despair.
Morning breath of progress reeked.
Going home was such relief,
I almost kissed the walls and door knobs
of our quiet country life. A couple grazing
in the grass, shaded by a sighing tree.
I took a shower, scrubbed so hard,
I heard the water's flesh like
hiccups stopping Sunday church.
Our next vacation would be real.
We would stay in ocean waves where
ruination didn't redden breathing flesh
or choke us with its wicked reins.

When Flaws Come Home

Who's Who in Hell.
Everyone sits around
in useless urgency,
waiting for candor's clamor
(it wears no shoes
and sneaks around).
Guilt is a pregnant volcano
and we are its rocks.
Money (which on earth
was cream for butter molds)
does not take down
the Windsor Castle of regret
for sucking on mistakes so long.
When earthly comes home to roost,
we inspect its nest
like a *Kleenex* for snot,
as if we might someday
earn the right to put stuff back.
God is a security guard
with his pants unzipped
who loses his credibility.

The Object Lesson

Summer spanked.
Reminding me
of times I didn't stop
to kiss the parted lips
of morning dew.
Steaming in the shade-less
grip of August suns,
I bolted like a wounded horse
to last gasp answers of the pool.

A palsied man on crosses twixt
a chair and gurney slapped
the ass of senseless whining.
Arms and legs were stunted sprouts
from old potatoes in a bin.
Head was ticking same as clocks.
Moved in such eternal cramps.
Tongue flapped sideways,
hanging out like soggy meat
that's falling through a paper bag.

His pain a catheter in place
to realizing inner-tubes.
I who griped of flattened tires,
aches attached to grocery shopping,
liners for my plastic limb like
condoms oversized exploding—
monsoon moaning at its finest—
met the object lesson's fire.

The Lonely Globe

You spin the globe of loneliness,
but cannot pierce its glassy frame.
Every weeping river rages—
makes your grieving fingers stick.
Booze brooms sweep the surface dust,
but do not touch dry dying's mud.
At sixteen years, I still see apples
on the tree—unbruised by aging ageless storms.
My day is made of tennis courts,
riding bikes, and "class dismissed!"
Suffer's not yet sharpened thorns,
except for stacks of surgeries.
Like Ping-Pong balls I flatten some,
but always seem to cross the net.
Fear is not a greyhound muzzled,
pinned in pens of starting gates.
There's water in the well out back.
I don't prefer a nap to life—
or feel the crust of crisis creme.

Your wife is rotting on the shelf
of cancer with its cupboards shut.
Her ovaries have turned to prunes—
knives must stomp and quick remove.
She locks away her cramps in piles—
sweaty socks for maids to wash.
You pace the den like mother bears—
anticipating preying wolves.
When living chokes and spits her out,
the oriental chill is there,
without the resignation part.
Black marble of the bathroom tile—
Satan's snakes one-upping smiles.
Death, a lump upon a globe;
art is architecture's ache;
mortal dares not read its map;
Sober is a *Magic Marker*
underlining hollow caves.

Achilles' Heels

Dirt was dry like flapjacks
burning on a griddle.
Whistles blew and traffic stopped.
I watched the train in chunky gasps
crawling over leather flesh.
Its boxes were a ribboned gift—
hands of ticking mortal clocks.
Plywood stacked in decks of cards,
our *Tinker Toys* of yuppie art.

A homeless man was paper wadded,
lying there beside the tracks.
His body in a tent of gray
like ashes flicked from cigarettes.
The bottle stuck in gravel pits
was charcoal on a barbecue.
Addiction is a, well, affliction,
hornets on a breast of chicken.
Never chosen, always there.
I was heading home to spoiled.
Maple-syrup moments dripping.
His was sweat like castor oil.

The bottle was a vacuum cleaner;
I had yet to plug it in.
Keyboards glittered in the grateful.
Tapping keys was sewing sequins
on a fancy evening dress.
Ulysses was a man in clay who
showed me where I might have gone.
Admission flows *ad nauseam:*
I couldn't even stop to breathe
the menthol of impending death.

Lampshades

Lampshades of a liquor store
that mellow broken, burning bulbs
with lights we've tried but can't reverse
by exercising tenderness.
A little boy you left for drugs
is rolling ditches of your life.
Drinking the venom that poisoned you,
smoking the pot that took you
for an evil spin and
never let you leave its reign.
If a conscience lives below defeat,
you'll change your ways.
He's chasing, you know,
desideratum's butterfly
by raw acquaintance with your sins.
He sees escape from prison walls
as joysticks for computer games.
He sees the money tree you grew as wits
at work and not despair's loud sad parade
that's looking for a checkered cab
to rescue what he cannot fix.

He sits alone on park bench thought—
considerate and screaming
silence to your ghosts with
visages he can't control.
Do you sweat the storms you left
with masturbating urgency?
Addiction is a lonely road
with gravel spitting everywhere.
You owe him room in passing lanes
to rev the engine past defeat.
Slug bait sprinkled on the lawn,
you've fed him to the squirming rats.
He clamors for approval's torch—
thirsts for love he cannot spell.
You've slaughtered pigeon innocence
and stolen all his fishing trips.
Stray bullets of dismissal's gun
you fired in empty wishing wells.

Adano's Bell in Syllables

A tired old jogger on beaten paths,
I scroll and stroll
through lists of words.
Letters melt lucidity,
wipe the sunscreen off my back.
Adano's Bell in syllables
that celebrate why battles start
in search of art and backward darts.
They all end up ammonia honest
not unlike those old latrines
in campgrounds with dynamic dumps
that promise lotion languishing
in languages connected to, contorted by
the presence of dream's rosaries.

My pen, a haunted house at times.
At others it's a German tank,
reminding me it owns my soul.
Knuckles cup as apple dumplings
cooling on a countertop.
A graveyard for the shells of nuts,
broken shoe-lace independence,
foot paths of a ghost's regatta
warming up for oceans crossed.

I order knowledge of myself
like rich desserts,
burning off time's calories.
You won't read a Pollyanna treatise here.
Pain exists in cactus flowers
tucked between both swords and thorns.
You won't see a war wrap up
and love the trash it rifles through.
Tons of warped old records stacked—
fond of notes they skid and skip.
Internal motion plays eternal.
Looking for lost jacket cause.

The Sign

Crouched in praying mantis style
among tuxedos in a can.
A gas tank of adrenaline
in bags that held a brittle straw.
You sat behind a cardboard plea:
"Homeless. Vet. Please Help.
God Bless." But he didn't.
And neither did we—as smart,
smart bombs of cars left marks
in ways they sandbagged fathomless.

Honest here was salad dressing
in bottles at a formal dance.
We weren't dressed to comprehend
in Saks Fifth clouds of grand conceit.
Words were masks for deadly demons
rifling through emotion's swamp.
Seaweed fingers held that sign—
covered eyes that knew too much,
came too close to whitened coal
in stomachs of a barbecue.
Old sardines among new lobsters
just before they dip in Hell.
See-through scarecrow penniless
chased money's peacocks down the street.
Spent seasons in a breakdown lane.
Ditches hugging hungry's grinch.

Red noses of your alcohol,
the only part of life we shared.
Umbilical cords that linked to ink
in ways truth spoiled holidays—
spots of blood in scrambled eggs
on silver platters of our lies.
Connections of camaraderie—
a rash of hemorrhoids born to hide.
Rigor's blood in terms of need
crosses classes in the dark—
looks the same on moon-less nights
in mortal's sour concert hall.

An Edge

When the cancer was gone
from the house and she was too—
ice-cubes popped from freezer trays—
there was no sunlight left to watch.
Just clouds that wailed in ardent grief.
The bonsais near the garden wall
did grow moss, but this was
green he couldn't touch.
His tongue just mucus on a leaf.
These dregs of wood
had elegance he couldn't spell.
Their bellies living off the rain.
The flower children all were hers.
They stood for how she
suffered so in a canyon
of silence too deep to cross
and still dropped pearls of dignity.
He paced the hall
like greyhounds itching
for a race, but starting gates
were always booze.
The bathroom was his favorite hole.
In ebony tile of mass despair.
Alcohol was water running on a cut,
diluting what it was to be.
It gave the poker chips of fate
an edge they did not own alone.

A Silent Sonnet

Strange. It was.
Summer's beriberi drought
with grape vines fried
in skillets of an August day.
Thorns were baby alligator teeth,
chomping straw of *might have been*.
Dirt stayed creases in a skirt.
Branches were a sewing kit;
we were groups of humble *Adam's*
stitching nervous clothes to wear.
The lot next door—a homestead
for these early dreams.
The big tree lounging on its side:
pirate pilots at its helm.

Green Peace wasn't politics,
but escalators to the clouds
and grass untouched by human plows.
The earth turned toast and all at once
the intangible maze of winter struck.
Brown went white. Hot suns withdrew.
We grew up faster than we planned.
The tree house leaves were
curtains frozen to the wood.
Trapdoors shut to fairy nowhere:
school pinched a nerve again.
Snowfall was a silent sonnet
sweeping attics with its hand.

Bourbon Street

Headline news:
a database of thick despair.
A homeless woman
left to die on stairways
of a parish hall.
She'd walked these streets
for two long years,
so much her visage vaporized.
Past beauty parlors, neon signs,
guarded chains of jewelry stores.
Beside a fancy restaurant.
White linen napkins in its bay—
all we had for sacrifice
was stained by ways we did not act.
Sensors of our windshield glass
were only tuned to private pain,
while universal grew like bugs
in urban's ugly petri dish.
In one long marathon of need,
she stood on toes of withered corks,
knocked on doors of have and grab
and hold and cold,
collecting hope in dented cans.
Bourbon Street stretched way too far;
a cobra curl of retrospect.
Her perish ran its sickly course.
Our candy canes, our vanes of greed
did nothing to unwind its coils.
The tank of human void was dry;
she a single stranded fish
in back seats of our fine sedans.
Beds of straw upon her head,
a rotted manger we ignored.

Apple Grief

The bonsai of straddled death
was a crew of nurses
catering all three meals
by injection with
glucose and morphine.
Both sugar, admittedly,
for fading sunlight.
I climbed a tree,
shook out angry apples
with seeds of cancer
by the hundreds—
steamed bitter into applesauce.
Took the bus
from school to you.
Brought you wishful Tupperware
but nothing meaningful to say.

Fruitcake flesh brought
grunts and sighs like
over-due library books that
no one wants to see or touch—
let alone take credit for.
That rickety fan blew
humid scents of final days;
a musty draft one finds at church.
The dresser with bottles
of perfume pills.
Stained-glass sorrow for my uncle;
pacing fevered cobblestones.
Hopeless wanted mercy booze
to help distribute helpless weight.
My applesauce, a joke (I know)
like feeding baby food to wolves.

Godiva Chocolate Rocks & Stones

It's a long title
for a long sin.
Poverty's shadows
are polka-dot dandruff
on velvet we brush.
The rebel network
of drawn shades
where wet tongues
bleed rust are hardly
welcome on the
easy side of granted tracks.
And the hospital truck
with a bed in its womb
is a corpse in the trunk
of our national car.
Pain rules night's
extended weight.

We pass by signs
"Will Work for Food"
like veins collapsed.
Drill for oil somewhere safe
where the homeless
don't roam and
faucets don't leak.
Away from the place
where *Godiva* chocolates
are piles of rocks—
just tents and shelters
from the plain wet rain.

The Money Moon

I memorized your favorite toy—
a ragged mutt with stuffing
poking through its seams.
A *Snoopy* always napping
just outside the range of wealth,
where all the pretty people lived.
You worshipped only Yuletide trees
that seemed to ache and needed love.
The kind without a stereo
in ribboned paper at the base
or Sycamores with tendons twisted,
growing sideways from the earth.
A tree house fashioned from a dream.
Your dog without a set of papers.
Just an orphan on the stage.

All at once too full of cash—
this saintly adoration died.
Inheriting a moon of money.
How it changed you, changed us all.
Up against the wall of greed.
The *S & M* of dollar signs
that stole the boy I loved beneath.
Now it's all Mercedes sports cars,
shirts in starch, and country clubs.
A mansion bigger than a castle.
Stock-trades, not a birthday card.
You pray to booze from five o'clock
until your tongue is etherized.
Children wander in your silence,
bounce on hope like rotted planks.
I hope it doesn't take a death
to caffeinate your modesty,
to bring you home to who you were,
a diamond in a septic tank.

The Hallmark Card

He graduated from Princeton
at the top of his class and went on
to a fine, fine medical school,
but years brought too much
helium of easy street;
he needed freight trains of defeat
to educate his leather heart.
Green masks were a lucrative choice
in many ways: they bought a safe
of step away, but blocked
his view of real trees.
Retorts to gut wrench agony:
"time is your friend...
this too shall pass."
We saddled up dismissal's horse.
Writing scripts for little pills
was wiping up a Noah's Flood
with nothing but a paper towel.
He needed tragic kidney stones
to force through urinary tracts.

Medicine craves, I'm sad to say,
required courses wrought
in dire desperation—
get real smart of being Black
before the swords of Ku Klux Klans.
Witnessing of bones meet saws,
tendons twisted, crammed in place
like corks in stale Chardonnay.
The kind of private agony
that freezes hair around our balls.
Dark, by sorrow's accident,
finds ways of beefing up the light.
He needed caffeine destiny
to fluff compassion's robe with fire.
His distance was a Magna Carta
smacking of a Hallmark card.

Quixote Winds

When I look in your eyes,
I see justice myths as empty urns.
Prometheus gave the world fire
and suffered for his sacrifice.
You are the boatman
of the River Styx, but
tragic vacuums swallow coins;
the truth of your moan
makes mortal deaf.

To help a friend,
you set up something worse
than death: a bullet
in your back for
every tender finger shared.
This year, Santa Claus
is a morphine drip
and enemas pour into a pile
of old nightgowns dropped
off like communion wafers
from someone who wants to
but cannot change despairing facts.

Nurses are your body guards.
Reindeer motion is nothing but thorns.
A hot, hot date with a water-bottle
and a row of bedsores
gone from red to black
like holly seeds the world ignores.
Christmas stockings are a joint.
An ambulance, your limousine.
Eggnog rhymes with *Lomatil*.
Through it all, there sings a muted
victory of how you put another first:
just like straw for eagle wings,
Quixote winds live in your hair.

For Julie Morgan, December 1998

The Bumper Sticker

"1st Battalion, 9th Marines, The Walking Dead"

Missives of pain beneath plain words.
We photographed that famous wall,
walked away as children from a broken toy,
no one came to meet your tears.
Dirt was crumbs of gingerbread—
mere mud in eucalyptus leaves.
Wisdom's beard was rearview mirrors;
I wanted you to rinse them clean.
Wondered if your mind still played
croquet with pails of planted bombs
and grass hut horrors up in flames.
You weathered hurricanes of death
but see through centers of their storms.

Embarrassed by our history books
like testicles that hang from shorts,
we look again at meat and miss
of battle cries. Wedding rice
was cooked in blood and served
with chopsticks of a myth.
Troops without that "Fruit Loop," sweet
mentality belonging to a soldier's youth.
Leveled by the arch of hell
in savage measures of a poem—
the kind that isn't written down
but lives with leeches in a swamp.
Courtrooms sat outside the war;
gavels met unknowing wood.
Cheeks of missions spat you out.
Metals seemed like paper airplanes
falling in a toilet's cup.

Shoe Box Coffins

When love's fresh cherries
grew pits and you spotted those rocks,
and he grew mean, mean thorns
of cattail rage, there was nothing
to do but help your friend.
Seasons once were not the ticks
they are in terms of clinging pain.
For thirty years, a grateful goat
that ate the grains of destiny.
The showdown here would tar
your days with paint from
Satan's gravel pit.
Shot five times in the back
and saved by doctors dodging
scorpions that had already
delivered the deadly sting.
To them, the end was an ambush.
To you, a shoe box coffin
trembling with releasing lids.

The body cast of paralyzed,
the only Christmas sock you own.
Your life is *Wild Turkey* now.
Motion's mission is the tilt
of your head and slow, slow
drips of dry wax tears.
Talcum shakes of discontent.
Torrential rains of fight insane.
Drugs are rising alligators
caught in clumps of quicksand time.
Poetry's a frail retort
to bridal suites of raping guns.
The praying mantis sacrifice
that ate the contents of your life.
The lambaste of your murdered dreams
in retrospection's cobra curls.
Anger is a floating phone booth
caught in floods of closet death.

Nazi Lampshades

College, for the most part,
had forgettable stones:
Milton, Tolstoy, Shakespeare suns.
Gibraltars of deep literature
sailed tall above my head.
Arnold's melancholy sea was
cardboard in its old complaints.
What stuck was Plath and Alice Walker,
Williams' ***Glass Menagerie***.

I was in a borrowed oven
turning up the role of gas.
Walker's eye shot bb guns,
returned them to their rightful slots.
Laura's limp was one I lived.
Each wore threads of separated
woven in among your braids.
Nazi lampshades of my flesh
in currents of forgiving light.
Emerald gloss of truth in thickets,
trout in back seats of a car.

Mind and body eating air—
flank steak sliced against its grain.
I could kiss their pages freely
long before I brushed my teeth.
A bubble bath in harbors of a funeral.
What stuck was slabs of human life
that studied red poinsettia leaves
and chilies split in earnest pain.
Horse thieves of dismissal's virus
tripping on the torch of grief.

Pill Bugs

Lamps and pillars made of guns—
pilot fish in time of war.
Teething sharks and mantras
of smug politics became
nice nuns who earned
the cloisters where they slept.
Barracks bumpered by a plan
for saving things, not
dying in a brother's arms.
Diaries of inner pillage
in a jacket handed down
from son to son as if it were
nice woolen suits and not
a stack of body bags
containing dreams of ruined fruit.

I think of ways your frail limbs
resented staid—represented
troubles of a universe—
hangnails hunting metal clips.
Pill bugs rolled in tiny balls,
reacting to the blessed danger
leaders touted then contorted.
Every goal you wore and bore—
pregnant promised birth of honor
tucked between sharp cactus blades.
Piñatas stocked with firm mistakes
heroes called an action verb.
Death's distillation always ruled,
taping every coffin shut:
firecrackers of our flags
were brittle, hot, and dangerous.

Bones & Borders

Yugoslavia: 1942.
A villa with its roses shot
like babies still in diaper shrouds.
Ice baths of a river's colon
could not stop the stand you swam.
Treading water in the Nile
with alligator penniless.
Your servants felled by rifle fire—
broken candles, bowling pins.
In the "land of the free"
you were pocket change,
but courage was your coat of arms.
Every gift you made or chose
had history woven it its seams.

You traded wealth for justice clouds.
Crossed the border in the night.
Sipping poor was broken glass.
Exchanging bricks for raw, raw clay.
The dribble of a legend flounders
held in hands you crossed for "right."
Broken English on your tongue;
a heart intact in every way.
The vigil was embracing life—
you cupped its cheeks and held it close.
The "wrong" is how you suffered cold
from those who thought themselves above.
A Yugoslav—a dignitary in your land.
Here, you were a mailman
who brought the need for freedom home.

December's Shade

Old age was a paper cut.
Death sat on a razor blade.
Sixty years of intimate.
Two circles made a single band.
December's shade pulled down in haste,
a Christmas fire this year is cold.
Your passing is a promenade
for seizures of my aching heart.
We weathered battle, peace as well.
A woman dies. A man remains.
The family tree is hollow now
without the ways you made it home:
nine-course meals with sips of wine;
warm that bit the chill in two—
our elbows frozen by the war.

My geriatric infancy at 87 tablets spent:
"I need you, need you, need you back."
Cilantro in the soup of art.
When guns and tanks had stripped our land,
we swam the river in the night.
Fingers turned to cubes of ice.
Will would be our only pick.
Liberty's statue seemed too tall.
Refugees of heaven lost
in nothing but our muddy clothes.
No language, no villa,
no roses, no job. Just hope
like dusty spiderwebs between
an attic's cracking walls.

If cash is a climate of faith in sand,
we made clay from penniless.
The occupation stole our lives—
left us mere discarded crusts.
The tenderness of crisis breeds
a legend bearing fruit in pain.
Our journey bruised by German tanks
as pears that dot an orchard's skies.
Your ears were always ripe with sighs
that heard and felt the bruising rain.

Wilted Marigolds

This nursing home—a misnomer
if ever one stood.
A prison camp with the
roiling boil of loneliness.
A singular fan crackling like
bacon in a skillet with holes.
The font of hugs was insincere.
Bubble baths with scented beads
drowned by that ammonia stench
from leaky pipes of catheters
in parables above our lives.

Compassion was the heroin
no one dared to seize or share.
Geriatric infancy—shoestrings loose.
A fall was just around the bend.
Those who could stuck fast
to motion's brittle light.
Leaned like wilted marigolds
on anchors of the safety rails.
Quick visitors were chocolate bars
and Don Quixote on a horse
that melted in the mouth of "old."
"Three Fountains" was "the best in town."
I wondered where the water was.

Fortune's Famine Visits Here

You lived the way a woman does.
Cleaning guns of sorrow's knives.
Hiking up hope's strapless bra.
Generous was dinner mints—
passed around without a word.
Patting disappointment's boils
with Kleenex of a patient ear.
Hauling luggage of regret
like pelicans with pouches stretched.
A man's volcanic temper spitting
lava rocks across a friend.
You went to help her pack her things—
pencil out a calm escape.
He shot you both, then shot himself.
He wore lucky death's eraser.
You are trapped in fortune's famine.
Morphine is your body lotion.
Bullets gutted seagull dreams.

Helpless is a scorpion.
There are no dregs of motion left.
Shrapnel is a shredding tongue,
since anger clearly rents your house.
Pity's puss is scalded milk
and indigestion's wrongful bricks.
I know you yearn for death's release
as winds that rule a dune of sand.
It is a gift I do not own
to give your end a birth of sorts.
Unzipped grief is all we share.
Hunch-backed sad is useless here—
like spreading pollen over snow.
I feed you fattening donut holes
against the doctor's warning bells.
Teeth are wolves cut loose to charge.
I have no change in clever pockets
save a flag of justice felled.

Serious Slots

It wasn't fun
to watch her lose,
take a drink,
lose a dollar,
take a drink,
lose another,
shake her purse
for anything.

Pot holes from
lit cigarettes—
silver blackened
desperate hands.
It wasn't fun
to watch her lose,
take a drink,
slip it in,
take a drink,
step off stairs
toward closing moons.

Avocado Issue Pie

Bruisable. Bright green. Lush.
This opening night
of brand new love.
Lights lit. Sweet sweat.
A spring in our hearts.
Cherry Jell-O on marshmallow nipples.
Then comes life. The knives.
Her stomach, once a cutting board,
fitness spreading the fragrance of envy,
warped by time and burning
in the acid of unpaid bills.
Faith browned too long
by the broiler of will:
a sunflower split, descending
in the dry crevasse.

Ribboned leaves of promises
that earthquakes of another slap,
another love (perhaps) assaults.
Curtains fall like finches
dropping from a telephone wire.
Cheesecake once,
our dreams were smooth.
Turn to avocado issue pie.
Badly blackened in the air
regardless of romancing seeds.
Slippery as otters on algae and moss
above a beating tide of flesh.
We stay to meet the suffer fork.
Swallow our choice to wafer ourselves—
as corks that never return
to the bottle the way they came.

Baby-sitting Bayonets

The silhouette of gravity
against the sky,
depression was your cup,
your bag, your pot of tea.
You made it ours.
We baby-sat your bayonets.
Only words, admittedly.
You killed the roots of decent jobs—
pigeons frying on a wire.
It had to do with attitude.
The way you slapped
affection's face was
much the same as cornered deer.
You grabbed. You stormed.
We ran. We scabbed.
Pneumonia was a brand of anger
passed along like winter colds.

Hope was snapped asparagus.
Never stayed in season long.
I bit back—exploding pens.
The misery of rust
and retrospect in frosting
caked by coughing winds.
Your little girls were
capillaries of the light—
but when they left,
we rode dead waves.
In flat cold practicality,
our wedding rings
made garbage ties.
Mud in snow of
once white trails.
I do not grieve our galaxy.
A ransom note for rising suns,
love's tuition climbed too high.

Lots of Practice Driving Ice

Wedding chimes turned tangled knots
when jobless stole what
little scraps of light we had—
harbors tucked away in albums
crammed beneath a sagging bed.
Marriage bloomed in nervous shades.
Hyde Park shrubs at midnight mass,
with no one out for company
except depression's practiced wolves.
Saber-tooth saws of words
were knives that had a place
in every pocket of the dark.
You judged the world as aphids
meant to steal a rose.
Every carrot fate I cropped
you splintered same as winter wood.
Divorce was merely semen crusted—
dried behind the fact of rape.

I burned you. You burned me.
The way you made us wear your need
like tennis shoes that didn't fit.
Smoke was, well, the only bird
that nested in our chimney flue.
We almost locked the sliding door
like switchblades snapped in self-defense.
Signing papers, summer breezes—
sledding down a mountain's neck.
I played what little cash I had
as fingers plugging saxophones.
Bitter's gristle—satin blessings—
set beside your silent vents.
I promised you my faithfulness.
Saddled up a cheerful horse.
Hooked oxen to a Christmas sleigh
since reindeer couldn't pull the weight.
The ice, of course, became so hard
that driving it got easier.
Booze became our slide trombone:
its oil thick as wet cement.

Some Soliel

Youth wrote
Sanskrit in the dirt,
signing up for
happy endings
same as letters
on a sweater—
looking for
a breast to cup.

Three days in bed.
Lost jobs.
Drawn drapes.
I mistook my
blindness
for a rainbow
and married you—
despite how loud
those sirens were.

Love's earring
quickly lost its back.
I pinned it on
with liquor's mount.
A pine cone frozen
to its earth.
Retrospect should
question jewels
even if they're jellyfish.

Some Soliel.
Same ol' mud.
Danubes of
depression's vice.
I did, I do, I dance
across report cards
of a cruel poem.
Our rings were
plastic bacon bits
that should have been
the real thing.

Your Exit

Your exit had an emerald's fire.
Green's my favorite color now.
The trees we planted in our minds
are toothpicks going after plaque.
The children of our marriage cold.
Money's menthol didn't help.
Laughter was a rippled nipple
poised as scented candles brewing
ways to change the chemistry
of love undone and left alone.
As radish flowers, it hid the sting
but didn't sand our texture much.
You can't plant shrubs in mud despair
and expect their bodies to stand up straight.
The same applies to little girls.
Anticipating perfect visits—
tailored suits you crammed
like *Skoal* in tiny cheeks.

Our sins were splintered bottles
in the trash my fingers kept returning to
as tongues around a broken tooth.
The booze was part to blame,
of course. I'll own up to pouring it.
But it was just the draft of skunks
and not the real animal.

Horror's Iceberg

An eight-year-old boy
was lost in the woods.
The snowy egrets of search teams
combed the hills of hopeless,
gone for days.
The father thought: "My kid's with you."
Grandpa thought: "He's with his dad."
Hunting for a Christmas tree,
the child became a chunk of human
blown through nostrils,
saviors hiccuped undeserved.

They hoped he'd fall in lava beds
and earth would shield him
from the freeze. Nature's quilt
not warm enough—
forget, forgive would never come.
Pneumonia bit the father's lip.
But prospects of his dying day
were nothing but a paper cut.
A city brushed the forest's web
with every gimmick in their palms.

Horror's iceberg on the news:
they found the boy—his parka
slabs of fruitcake wrapped
and gum-stuck to the hostile ground:
death determined holidays
would never pass their way again.
An accident where angels
do not seem to live;
where God does not exist at all;
where suns will be a chunk of ice;
their nerves removed by root canals.

The Font of Gin

I sparkled when I drank at first.
My buddy booze was stepping stones.
Warm release to giddy fruit.
Not the wrinkled, aching prunes
of memories that hurt to pass
like body bags in battlefields
or piercing giant kidney bricks.
The font of gin that stretches joy.
Softens porn intendingly.
Especially the undertows
in taverns of emotion's tome.

The bottle let me take a nap.
Getting high was candle snuffers.
Drinking was an easy way
to run away from suffer's home.
Chimeras turned to weeping pines,
sustaining roots of dignity.
Roman pillars, separation,
guarding gates of "feel this"
like soldiers with the news of death.
I soaked my heart in Chardonnay
for longer than I'd care to own.
My buddy booze, a jellyfish.
Invectives of regret would scream
like brutal stings of scorpions.

Blank Grief

In Loving Memory of Margaret Kurtz Buck

The statue of Mary in white,
white stone is inches away
from your quiet grave.
Grass is long around its lip.
I'm ashamed I do not know
for sure what day and year
the cancer won, reduced
your frame to apple cores.

I just assume seasons
jumped from summer
to ten winter months.
Your smiles in
tiny picture frames
are lipstick smothered
stoic curves.
I'd guess them
tusks of elephants as ivory
and as dense as love.
I wonder what you
thought of me—
born in teething tragedy
you hadn't time
to brace in change
or fix by turning
screws of faith.

Legs in crusts of body casts.
Baby booties, cruel jokes.
The ache you own
of losing me is matched
by my imaginings.
I have no concept who
you were—Father's grief
removed his tongue.

Splitting Suffer

Acrid caves of slipping motion
pushed me through these sliding doors.
Ammonia clean was drying piss.
The starch of sheets in sterile white.
Ski-masks—icons of a mugger—
pressed around indignant ears.
I'd have crawled through canyons
lined with tumbleweeds to
take a step without a walker.
Fading health, a praying mantis
dining on the dregs of frail.

"Replacing hips is quite routine,
but one is all she has in hand.
She will have to bear the weight.
The other choice, a wheelchair."
That option was a felony
and I would never go to jail.
I stood on metal, grafted joints
like soggy concrete barely set.
Veins of dread were varicose—
smelly strings of sauerkraut.
I rode on wings of Demerol.
Flesh became a broken plate.
My family came to visit twice.
Left an iris on the mattress—
lily pads in jungle swamps.

Hacienda hope was bombed.
We were huddled in its bunkers.
Sperm in search of ovum strength.
My gaping gown a parachute
with cords that wrapped around us both.
All night long immersed in torture.
Squirming bass in poachers' boats.
Siamese twins of splitting suffer
sculpted like an ivory cane.
You fed me what the others couldn't:
spoons of ice for boiled madness.
Love was blizzards set in June.
You supplied the winter coat.

Candor's Animated .gif

Certain items scream and claw
to be contained: poetry is one of them.
Its license (no matter how dearly, clearly,
tearly learned) must connect
with others' maps around the globe.
It's a hideous thought to go unread.
There you are in deep-ends
of a swimming pool:
someone grabs emotion's hair,
holds it under beating waves
where choking is the gasp of art.
Rabid, rapid fire of need
becomes the only oar in reach.

Take pity on my crisis creme.
A stream of desperation's semen
lined with rocks that shift themselves.
No such thing as steaming milk
diluting rust of where I've been.
An oriental loneliness that spreads
in parchment paper fans.
Charlatans of all my flaws
in shades of blood I did not choose,
so please be kind to open wounds.

Black marble of an inner chill
comes in contact with the sky—
becomes an alabaster egg
or tofu craving seasonings
of turquoise painted "prove" and "save."
Respect my frames like Scrabble squares
that must sometimes invent a word.
Sorrow's meat is donut holes:
they had a place, but lost their caves.
Walk carefully on slippery floors;
keep the lid on judgment salt.
Candor's animated .gif will
always have a flag to raise.

Absolutely Tender Corn

The dip below the current smiles.
Berry seeds of very buried who
she was beneath balloons and
courage pouncing mountain lions.
The smack, the whip was artistry.
The victim here was not a victim really.
Sensing this, he curled his arms
around the saddle of her pride.
Beads of sweat he wiped away.
Love was such a rising choir
that no one could mistake its song.

The barnacles of bathroom mirrors
would fasten just like buttons
double-knotted by the eyes and
bibles bound in “rise above.”
A Mormon when it came to faith.
Over-dressed and inner-awkward.
Amputated bones were hard-
to-broach anathemas and
she had luggage full of scorn.

Her flesh was new to negligees and
strobe lights on accepting thrones.
She would wiggle in their bed
like rodents cornered by the light.
Lifting gently, watching
for the underneath.
Years were husks and she was ears
of absolutely tender corn.

The Surplus Store

This shame an almost witch's spell.
Meant to steam like winter fog
until a sunrise interferes.
Find a place to carve itself
on tomes of years that sat and sat,
stretched and stretched,
a Buddha in a yoga pose
that looks for incense in the wind.
Surplus here was not
attached to army boots,
unless you'd draw connections here
between the slant of bossy will
and squeezing limes of acid fate.
Seaweed dregs of yardsale bones
caught in nets of itching try.
Amputation's vacuum bag.
I was just exploding dust.

Chicken stock with greasy curses;
losing love was one of those.
Flaws would have their way with me
like bees that land on chicken breasts.
The sty in the eye of the River Styx
was rhyming and removing slurs.
Bookends for this pilgrimage—
the chutzpa of your loving arms.
Struggle's slime to peel and scrub—
brown spots on a celery stalk.
Without them, I'd be sliding fast:
the race of drag and drop would crash.
I'd be a pile of pages, yes,
but stripes around a body bag
without much purpose in my hands—
ambition's pen would be a drought;
pencils standing tall today would
match the crush of broken chalk.

The Real Thing on Fishing Poles

Rainbow arch aphasia love.
Anticipation's lather blather
filling up a root beer mug.
I kiss you quickly—
hanging onto summer heat.
When eyes meet 'yes'
and drop one 'e'—
bury sewers of divorce—
putting up log cabin walls that
match a forest's pine perfume.
When silence feels like tennis shoes.
When apertures of loneliness
are widows minus poison spots.

Suns are such sweet tangerines.
Tantivy trust becomes
warm blankets over flesh.
All these little notices
blending license passion earns.
We both paid tolls—
bought tickets to our closing plays.
Now we live above all acts—
thumbtacks finding firm for corks.
A pasture full of ocean pearls
I stroke but dare not analyze.
I hear the squeak. I hear the snap.
The real thing on fishing poles.

The Titanic & the Iceberg

We share, in a way,
a capsule of immiscible love.
I have not the sort of bones
one takes home to the table
for Christmas Dinner.
To meet the meat of stampeding hooves
dialing in judgment from a touch-tone phone.
“She has only one leg?” Aghast. Gassed.
Out of kindness, curtain silence falls.
I drink pity for breakfast
and vomit its remains with will.
Drop my single foot as a stick in the ground—
drive it hard to stake a tent of grace,
which vacillates from weak to worse.
I have stacks of stories, all horrific:
they’ve grafted and drafted and whittled my limbs
until there is barely room for another knife.
What lies beneath these leather scars
are daisies crushed, sand dollar dreams
and the chalk of fury lathered
by the wild call of proving my worth.

Tender bubbles beneath my skin
have not been touched, because.
I’ve been tripped, duped, tied
by stares and stairs.
I climb them, when I can,
in the darkness of backs turned,
so my limp is leveled by the
pageant of their silk ballet.
Bubbles proceed to fly, but
only where it is safe
and that is in your arms.
Ours is not greeting card love—
with stickers of poise on ballroom floors.
But a smacking, sacred kind:
dodging the sting of defeat;
two hummingbirds tapping out sweet spots
of plain brown-wrapper tragic times.

Mints on Muddy Pillow Shams

Diogenes in a hot tub of curdled dreams,
I tinker with emotion's safe.
Nylon stockings of a lyric
hide my flesh but call it up.
Judgment dandruff mixed with snow.
The apple rots from inside out.
For many years my only salve—
a shot glass with its line respected.
God, I held that ether well
like chlorine poured in swimming pools.
Something snapped. Sheets went stale.
Sad passed out, got stinkin' drunk.
I was robbing myself without regret
or knowing how much cache was gone.
I'll tell the plain brown-wrapper truth:
train wrecks on the rails of wine
took semi-trucks and made them small
like Matchbox Cars in Christmas socks.

Pillbox words in stanza wallets
take the heat I used to drink.
Ghosts and cobwebs suck their breath
from cloisters of my whittled bones.
Belittled, befuddled, be agony's fire.
For nearly twenty winter years,
mints upon my pillowcase
were bottles emptied for escape.
I know I should have prayed instead,
but God would surely understand
how pain can rape a midnight mass.
The pillar monk of crippled tides
was sadly sealed off from wise.
Crusoe on the cross of pain,
I wonder wander courage caves.
Sing Sing out of key but there.
Shame sham concentration leads.
Sober's closet sees the dark for what it is
and somehow corners breaking light.
Liquor's penitentiary was holding cells
for "do not touch me with the night."

Steaming Grief

As masses on the tail of death,
this Sunday in the August heat
wore cold, cold chills of losing you.
What hair you had was way past gray—
white wafers of a gibbous moon.
Your will grenades—their metal tired—
I gave you mine in rocking chairs
beside goodbye I couldn't stop.
IV hope; retreating veins.
A morphine drip—the only way
my father (a doctor) could stir this mess
or touch the boil of sorrow's steam.

Lipstick striped the counter's edge.
Its crayon broke when legs collapsed.
The talcum dust of memories
besieged the air and your elbows
to which I've clung these forty years
became a Venus to paint with words.
You had every right at 90 years
to slide asleep but I pulled you back
with selfish need like saviors
drowning in their blood: shucking clams
of "Damn it all! I want you back!"
Waved Dickinson in sepia
across your cheeks to fan
the lyrics of your ways.
Pounded sonnets in your ear
to warm a washcloth for your head.
I puked until the grieving left and then
returned as lights in fog
that smack stray cats in search of food
and tiny rays of human warmth.

Emotion Rang

Teaching Steinbeck would be easy.
After all the theme was clear.
Elisa's story was of passion
meeting silence, turtle doves
that hit a brick wall mind and all,
its feathers, all its urges needing
stuffing, washing, scrubbing hands of
dreams that would, no never could,
sprout blossoms of a cherished child.

Yellowed notes in front of me
lay quiet as unopened tombs.
Purple flowers in the margins.
Doodled art that smelled of blood.
I started out with all intention,
sticking to the story's glue.
A student in the class collapsed
and jetted from the smoky room.

She knew I knew, I knew she knew.
Sandbags of our destitution,
barren wombs that froze and wept when
someone touched "Chrysanthemums."
"It wasn't fair" was rolling marbles in
our eyes that somehow fell upon the page.
We wrote our answers to the test.
They were not of right and wrong.
Issue sweeping brooms of ink that bled
in ways our tongues had fought.

Pens were knives of fate so callous.
No such thing as seedless melons
in a juicy thinking camp.
The summer was too hot to handle.
Class dismissed before the bell.
Emotion rang its clanking hollow.
We would have to answer it.
Teaching Steinbeck, well, was easy.
Learning it was not.

Hornets at a Barbecue

Typos on the filtered glass.
Sulking flies on summer screens.
I want and need a poem to shriek.
To slice your ear as others have.
The "yes" critique is jingle bells
but we aren't courting Santa Claus.
You tell me where the stanzas shake.
I tumble down the stairs agreeing.
The size and squeeze of syllables.
Puzzle pieces dodging measure
same as busy eagle wings.

Form is, well, cilantro leaves
with scents of lilac unexplained.
Overkill is barking dogs.
Excess will announce itself
like bookends sliding down a shelf.
You read and weep and write your own.
Brush away clichés and all,
our hornets at a barbecue.
A writer on a writer's back.
Communion wafers in a cave.
We taste and pass the art along.
Children looking for the notes
in harbors of a rising choir.

Arrivederci to the Blues

Dead letters still so much alive as
weeds that sprout between two yards
despite the fences wrought of pining
places in our hearts we know
are better nailed shut.
Our wedding album gathers dust.
"Out, out damn'd spot." Photos
just like close-up shots of rapids
in a river turning angry at the edge
of yet another setting sun.

A dozen years have passed in sand.
Still the same, you blew us out
like candles on a birthday cake,
because you found another victim,
brighter shades of tulip lips.
You asked me once if poetry I
wrote of love, it sprang from us,
the answer is the honest gristle
of a tear that there was not enough
to lay in tombs of empty pages here.

The love I thought we had in hand
was just your very selfish fist.
Sorrow's blood is like a clot.
You bump it and it bleeds anew.
Our song is now a funeral dirge.
It is a knife, I'll grant you that.
But closure's irony has passed.
This a, yes, surprising twist.
Arrivederci to the blues.

Raccoon Understanding Eyes

Pain, an often homeless wound:
a common bass we size and toss in
choppy seas of someone else's continent.
Thermal knowledge of the dark I've
never shared with anyone.
Raccoon understanding eyes
you toothpick open when I can't.
Every step I try to take:
a ticket to the lottery.
Sometimes win. This time lose.
I hit the ground like ice-cubes split
with picks on slippery countertops.
Crock pots steaming with the worst—
you drove the state at 95
on nothing but adrenaline.
The fiddle of my severed leg
beside your well-tuned violins.
Agony to work around and then remove
with utter care like urns behind museum glass.

Men before you, scrambling crabs
when pain came through in German tanks.
Peeing on a summer lawn—
this brand of candor wasn't done.
My Rolodex of bones complain;
you listen to their rhapsody.
Our passion's testament at work.
I rock in the seat of our old sedan:
as close as I will ever come
to slamming fists against a wall;
chewing hope that pain will lift
like taffy in the jaws of dogs
that isn't going anywhere.
If dread is blue exploding pens,
then both our shirts are flooded here.
Our cherish Stradivarius I
wouldn't trade for Noah's Ark.
When fated mountains turn their backs,
your burst of sunlight just appears.
The *coup de grace* of medicine
is not this winter's rising sun.

Swinging Doors

The only humanoid I've ever dragged—
dreading, beheading shopping for shoes—
is ***minimize*** and busy shoehorns
of a tongue to cram my flesh
in pre-existing smooth canoes.
I have no oars of understand how
leather and heels can mean so much.
Bite so hard. Drown so fast.
Breakers in a choking sea.
Faith is closer to mesquite than
clean air drafts from summer decks
that crumble as I travel them.
"Anatomies of challenges build character..."
Leave It To Beaver re-run tapes
for lucky legs that cross and play
like well-connected batteries.

My surgeries maimed other men—
became a flight of stairs too steep.
I'm far less brittle in your arms—
a poet with apparent depth
that plows ahead through oatmeal fog.
A pasture full of peonies
that roll wet walls of cripple's Louvre.
I dance between a windmill's blades.
Knowing how such risk can bleed.
Smelling fear like wet manure.
Trusting in the space to move.
We talk as roses opening
in palms of concentrated light.
Collecting tears of melted ice,
you treat the need for tenderness
as swinging doors that have the power
to fell a stand they need to launch.
Bleeding beets of pounded stumps
have grown by threads beyond their blush.
You pull out chairs to seat long scars
in ways I thought impossible.

Assumption

It's been two years, one month, three weeks,
four days.
Since I sat on the edge of her bed
reading "Dover Beach" aloud
for ears pressed firmly
to the final page of life.
Patches of strength
curling their corners
like Band-Aids over wetted skin.

And I thought I could.
Make crepes that smiled from the pan
and press her Irish linen
without the steam of tears
and tuck it out of sight.

We matched like new pairs of socks
in my underwear drawer
or widows holding hands at Sunday Mass.
I'm sure she knew I smoked
and never said a word.
But turned faux pas like broken lips
of china cups around to face the wall.
It's been two years, one month, three weeks,
four days.

And I thought I could.
Sit on her bathroom floor alone.
Use wine to take me places I needed to go.
She had this way—
of revising defeat—
of pouring waterfalls of misery
into margarine tubs
and sending me home,
steering straight.

I still feed the daisies she left
with watered gin, and they flower
even in September's shade.
Each book she bound with patient flesh.
Advice a gilded potpourri
sprinkled like sugar
over bowls of regret.

We both agreed that bridge
was a waste of precious hours.
That poetry and shoehorns
wedged crippled toes
into the "best of times."
It's been two years, one month, three weeks,
four days.

And I thought I could.

Architecture's Reason Fire

The doll house was a masterpiece
you stroked and sculpted in the night.
When I was six, its ambiance was
walls and paint and furniture.
You were childless. I was yours.
Holidays would burn the most.
Your "Sunday Brightener" in a ball.
Excuses for a batch of cookies.
Came in blasts, then rolled away.
Stealing weekends back from empty.
Borrowed children—bands of sorrow
snapped at times like soggy towels.

As fertile soil will court a weed,
elbowed fate has razor edges.
Here a woman born of turquoise,
brittle stars of coral reefs
to be a set of golden prongs:
patient, funny, morals of Gibraltar's size,
recited to the vacant clouds.
Ship-wrecked oars in driftwood scabs
that crusted in the August sun.
Your breasts were huge and so are mine
from having just too much to give.
Thank you notes I learned from you.
They had to be such iron skillets
scorching when they touched your hand.

A hyacinth that roots in darkness,
you were gracious. I am not.
Toilet-training rancor's cat
to leak upon the empty page.
Some thirty years beyond our bond,
I fathom every empty cave
you had the love to rifle through.
This poetry is sour milk
of sadly silent mommy chimes.
Envy's smoke rings in the air
around a summer barbecue.

Few Angels

Rich rarely fathoms
the silk of its wings.
Its schoolhouse
must be built from poor
and pounded nails
of struggle flames.
The world is wounded
and saved by shades
of capability, but
our angels are
too few, too fat
to squeeze through
poverty's cracks
and we hoard
the can of silver polish
as well as the metal
of love itself.

The Pipe of Grief

Christmas morning's muddy snow
in stockings that I couldn't hang.
The day you died was ultra-violet
desperation coming back to visit me.
I balanced on the raft awhile,
licked the sucker isolation,
lost an oar and guzzled wine.
It was all I had for Kleenex.
Hadn't quite expected torrents,
poisoned joy so thirsty, dry that
matches would have been an angel.
All the glitter on the tree was
brighter than my eyes could handle.
Holidays were felonies without
your hands to pat them down.

Tinsel on the pining fur
was sagging as I spoke of you.
The ornaments you made yourself
slipping from its weathered branches.
Aiming fire at God, at fate,
I ran the gamut cleaning house.
Pressed your Irish linen twice.
Waited for the whispered steam
to tell me I had I missed a spot
or folded napkins inside out.
Ninety years, you'd had enough
of motion's meager brittle wreath.
Infernos on the stage of death
are hunchbacks with a harpsichord.
Wrenches of a rolling stanza
couldn't fix the pipe of grief.

Popped Umbrellas

Since my first marriage
had the flavor of old bubble gum.
Since my second was musical
chairs of a prison camp.
The only treeline being that
of need and deep sea dire
depressing tides where smiles
broke rules and were not tolerated,
where temples of tempers
stole cushions from hearts
and sex went solo, sadly enough.

I had a number of serious
sentence fragments
when it came to willing.
Of course, when love drifts by,
you jump on without much choice,
like a moving sidewalk
that jets toward joy
you just can't stop.
Dread's designated driver
gets drunk and you don't mind much.
Old brown boxes of sour fairy tales
are overdue library books
in the back seat of an old sedan,
so you return them shyly
and proceed as hummingbirds
that respect the flutter
of passion's heated wings.

Love's hieroglyphics
are kin to honeydew:
you just sense when
the season is right and slit it
when the moment strikes.
And we did.
Touchdowns came so naturally.
Umbrellas popping to meet clean rain.

About the Author

Janet Buck holds a Ph.D. in English from Oklahoma State University and teaches writing and literature at the college level. Her poetry and poetics have appeared in ***The Melic Review, The Pittsburgh Quarterly, 2River View, The Rose & Thorn, Pyrowords, Disquieting Muses, Perihelion, Southern Ocean Review, Savoy, The Horsethief's Journal, The Suisin Valley Review, In Motion, The Recursive Angel,*** and hundreds of journals world-wide. In 1998 and 1999, she has been a featured poet for ***Seeker Magazine, Poetry Today Online, Vortex, Conspire, Poetry Cafe, Dead Letters, the storyteller, Athens City Times, Poetik License, 3:00 AM e-zine,*** and ***Carved in Sand***. Her poetry has received awards from ***Orpheus Press, Kimera, Poetry Heaven, Gravity, Voyager Publishing, Poetry Super Highway***, and ***Black Butterfly Press***, and she was a juried poet for the '99 Houston Poetry Fest in October. Buck is one of ten poets from around the globe to be featured at the "One Heart, One World" Exhibit at the United Nations Exhibit Hall in New York City in April, 2000. Her poem "Acrylic Thighs" will be translated into five languages and paired with original artwork. The tour will travel to France, Australia, Vietnam, and Japan and be an integral part of the Paralympics next year.